My War

Prisoner of War

Stewart Ross

HODDER
Wayland

an imprint of Hodder Children's Books

**This book is dedicated to Niel Nye, who sadly died in January 2003,
just months before his story was due to be published.**

Produced for Hodder Wayland by
Discovery Books Ltd
Unit 3, 37 Watling Street, Leintwardine, Shropshire SY7 0LW

First published in 2003 by Hodder Wayland, an imprint of Hodder Children's Books
This paperback edition published in 2005

British Library Cataloguing in Publication Data
Ross, Stewart
Prisoner of war. - (My war)
1. World War, 1939-1945 - Prisoners and prisons - Juvenile literature
2. Prisoners of war - Juvenile literature
I. Title
940.5'472

ISBN 0 7502 4212 4

Printed in China

Series editor: Gianna Williams
Designer: Ian Winton
Picture research: Rachel Tisdale

Hodder Children's Books would like to thank the following for the loan of their material:
Bettmann-Corbis: 18; Corbis: 8; Hulton-Deutsch Collection/Corbis: 19; Hulton Getty: *cover* (main picture), 6, 10, 11, 16 (both), 21, 25, 26, 27; Robert Opie: 23.
Cover: Hulton Getty (main picture), smaller photograph from the personal collection of Robert Coles.

Discovery Books would like to thank the following for the kind loan of their material:
Len Baynes, Niel Nye, Robert Coles, Stan Whittaker and Jean Arger.
Excerpts and photographs from Len Baynes' book *Kept – The Other Side of Tenko* reproduced with kind permission of the author.

Hodder Children's Books
A division of Hodder Headline Limited
338 Euston Road
London NW1 3BH

Contents

The Worldwide War

Britain and France entered the Second World War on 3 September 1939. They were among the Allies (eventually including Russia and the USA) fighting against the Axis powers of Germany, Japan and Italy.

Allied soldiers, sailors and airmen fought in many different parts of the world. Military personnel from both sides were captured and held prisoner until the end of the war. Well over 120,000 soldiers, sailors and airmen from Britain, its Empire and Commonwealth were taken prisoner.

LEN BAYNES

Len was born in Hertfordshire in 1919 and joined the reserve Territorial Army aged 19. He was one of the 16,000 British prisoners of war taken in Singapore in 1941 and was a Japanese PoW until August 1945.

NIEL NYE

From Bromley in Kent, the Reverend Niel Nye joined the Royal Air Force as a chaplain. He was captured by the Germans in North Africa, handed over to the Italians, escaped and returned to the RAF. He remained with the air force until 1946.

This book tells the remarkable stories of five of these prisoners of war (PoWs): four British and one Frenchman.

ROBERT COLES

Bob Coles was brought up in Northampton. He joined the RAF as a volunteer in 1939. After crashing into the sea off the coast of Holland, he was taken prisoner and spent the rest of the war in German PoW camps in Germany, Austria, Poland and Lithuania.

STAN WHITTAKER

Stan was born in 1925 in Kent. After serving in the Home Guard, at 18 he joined the army and entered a parachute regiment. Landing in Holland in 1944, he was captured and remained a PoW until freed in 1945.

JEAN ARGER

Born in France in 1918, Jean was doing national service when war broke out. He was captured as the Germans invaded France in 1940 and spent the rest of the war in German PoW camps. After being held by the Russians, he eventually returned to France in June 1945.

Joining Up

The outbreak of war in September 1939 came as no surprise. Even so, it was a frightening time for most people.

From June of that year, British men over 18 were being called up into the armed forces. Some joined as volunteers.

▶ Ready for war – young men were called up, or 'conscripted', for military service more than four months before the outbreak of war.

STAN

I didn't have enough education for the RAF. I joined the infantry and we did training in Beverley, Yorkshire. I enjoyed it – what you made of it depended on you. Then I volunteered for the Parachute Regiment. Someone from the village was in the Paras, so I thought it might suit me.

Volunteers chose whether to join the army, navy or air force, although they were not always accepted by the service of their choice. Conscripts normally had to go where they were sent. All new recruits began service life with a period of training.

LEN

Most of us were pleased and pretty excited at the prospect of seeing the world. As we were issued with tropical kit we assumed we were off to North Africa. In fact, after calling in at Halifax (Canada), Trinidad, Cape Town and Bombay, still without a clue where we were to finish up, we arrived in steamy Singapore.

JEAN

In August 1939 I was at Versailles with the 22nd Artillery Battalion. I had been doing my National Service since November 1938. All men had to do two years National Service from the age of 20. Nobody liked it much — it was just my bad luck to be doing it when war broke out!

▶ Bob Coles in flying gear during his training with the Royal Air Force.

Capture!

Soldiers were taken prisoner when there was no point in fighting on or when their commanders ordered them to surrender. Airmen, mostly bomber crew, were captured when they were shot down or crashed while flying over enemy territory.

STAN

The attack came in on a group of us. Luckily all the firing missed me. We just put our hands up. There was nothing else to do.

Most British prisoners were taken in three campaigns. The first, when the Germans swept across northern Europe in the spring and summer of 1940. At Dunkirk, northern France, in May and June 1940, 34,000 British soldiers were captured; a few weeks later the Germans took some 1.5 million French PoWs.

◄ Defeated and depressed, British and French PoWs are led from the Dunkirk beaches to long years of captivity in German-occupied territory.

BOB

We were flying low over Holland to avoid enemy ships and aircraft, we climbed suddenly and our plane's tail hit the sea. The next thing was a terrifying impact.

We were met by an officer and half a dozen soldiers armed with tommy-guns which they aimed at us. We raised our hands, they surrounded us, patting us to search for weapons.

▲ Bob's painting of his aircraft on the night it crashed.

The second campaign was in North Africa, where British troops fought Italian and German forces from 1940 to 1942.

The third campaign was in Asia, when the Japanese invaded British territories such as Singapore during 1941 and 1942.

NIEL

Our retreating forces were bottled up in Benghazi, North Africa. I saw a road block half a mile ahead and drove forward to investigate. It looked like an innocent farmhouse, but I suddenly realized it hid a camouflaged German tank. Just as I dropped flat on the ground, a shell blew my car to smithereens! The tank stopped a yard or so from me, the lid popped up and a German officer shouted. I had no choice but to surrender – so glad not to have been flattened!

Name, Rank, Number

In 1929 a number of Western nations had signed the Geneva Convention stating that PoWs were to be treated humanely. It said that PoWs were permitted to tell their captors only their name, rank and number. (All service personnel had a unique identification number.)

◄ No escape — German paratroopers stand guard over captured British soldiers, June 1940.

LEN

I got the greatest shock of my life when a messenger came up and told us we had to surrender. Up to then we thought we were holding our own. A little later the Japs came out of the trees surrounding us. We were herded off to a nearby tennis court. We soon realized that for the moment at least we weren't going to be shot, and so we began to stake out our spot to spend the night. We all just about found ourselves room to lie down, albeit like sardines.

The Convention also said PoWs were to be adequately fed, clothed and housed, and were to have access to medical attention. Visitors from neutral countries were to check that the Convention was being followed.

Neither Russia nor Japan had signed the Convention.

▼ Behind barbed wire, British PoWs captured in North Africa are being transferred to camps in Italy.

JEAN

We were ordered to surrender when the French government came to terms with the Nazis. The Germans held us in Colmar [in eastern France], keeping us in barracks. We were quite comfortable. But two months later we were loaded into uncomfortable cattle trucks and taken, non-stop, to Germany.

The Camp

Prisoners of war were held in camps. These ranged from ancient fortifications, such as the famous Colditz Castle in Germany, to wooden huts surrounded by barbed-wire fences. Each hut housed as many as 50 men sleeping in bunk beds. They were usually freezing cold in winter and stifling hot in summer. The prisoners themselves were responsible for keeping them clean.

BOB

After our grilling [questioning] we were moved into the tiny barbed-wire compound. I shall never forget that awful feeling of confinement when I first found myself hemmed in on all sides by barbed wire, watched over by guards on raised platforms with machine guns and searchlights.

▶ Bob's painting of the inside of a prison camp hut. There are numbers on each bunk bed, as well as graffiti.

Many camps were situated in remote places. This made it difficult for prisoners who escaped from the camp to get away. Prisoners were frequently moved from camp to camp to foil escape plans.

LEN

My first impression of the camp was filth and chaos. The huts that we were going to live in still had the rubbish of the people who had been there before us strewn about, and the camp itself was a sea of mud.

Camps shared the same features as prisons – high walls or fences, barbed wire, searchlights and continual patrols by guards, often with dogs.

▲ The flimsy wooden huts of the Kanburi Camp, Thailand, where Len was held by the Japanese. The building in the foreground is the cook house.

NIEL

After a month a new order was issued removing all officers of major/squadron leader upwards, so I was taken to Piacenza in northern Italy. This was an ex-convent, immaculately clean but with only a small garden to exercise in.

Weak with Hunger

Food was scarce during the Second World War, particularly for PoWs. In every country the needs of the civilian population always came before those of prisoners.

Occasionally food aid parcels from the Red Cross got through. In Japanese and Russian camps, many PoWs literally starved to death.

▼ As camp photographer, Bob captured many aspects of PoW daily life. Here PoWs queue for a meagre meal.

▲ Hungry men in Bob's camp stare down at their rations of swede peelings.

Poor diet meant poor health. PoWs generally had inadequate medical attention and camps were short of basic medicines. Furthermore, particularly in Japanese camps, the toilet facilities were often revolting. This led to epidemics of diseases like dysentery.

LEN

Instead of clean latrines [toilets], we had shallow trenches which writhed with maggots. There were several thousand of us in the camp, but only one tap for water; this was allocated to the cooks for two-thirds of the day. If anyone wanted a wash it meant queuing up for most of their spare time.

▶ Len while in hospital recovering from the injuries he received while trying to defuse a bomb.

JEAN

After a while fellow prisoners who were working on farms improved our meals by smuggling in fresh produce, such as eggs. Sick PoWs were examined by the camp doctor, a German. There were few medicines. Serious cases were admitted to hospital, but this was rare.

Work

For most PoWs every day was the same, starting with a parade and roll call and ending with all prisoners being confined to their sleeping quarters after dark.

▲ Forced labour for PoWs — Polish prisoners are made to clean the railway tracks at Thorn station on the German–Dutch border.

▲ British soldiers escorting Italian PoWs from their makeshift camp to their place of work. Several of the British soldiers have swapped their steel helmets for more suitable sun helmets.

STAN

I was made to work because I wasn't an officer. We worked at a railway yard, building a boiler house. We didn't mind the work because we knew it would never be finished before the war ended.

The Geneva Convention said officer PoWs could not be made to work. Men of other ranks spent their time in captivity doing tedious manual labour. As the Japanese did not hold to the Convention, by the end of 1943 they were expecting all ranks to work. Their most notorious project was the Burma Railway. Thousands of Allied PoWs died on this 'Railway of Death', a Japanese scheme to build an overland link between Thailand and Burma using PoW labour.

LEN

The Japs [the Allies' nickname for the Japanese] turned us out for work at daybreak. We were working on a railway embankment that was some 20 feet high. The earth had to be carried up to the top by hand. As we still had to shift the same amount of earth per man as when the embankment had been lower, we really did have to work flat out to finish by the time it got dark. After slaving in the tropical heat all day with little to eat or drink and few breaks, in the evenings we staggered back to our camp with trembling legs.

◀ A drawing of the British PoWs building a railway embankment on the infamous 'Railway of Death' in Burma.

The Guards

The guards at most PoW camps were generally soldiers who were not suitable for front line action. Many were over 40 or had some slight disability.

BOB

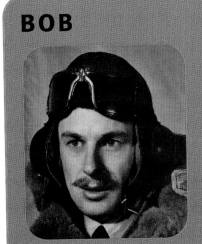

Speaking reasonable German, I had cultivated one good contact, an elderly guard, and in exchange for cigarettes he would supply such things as bread, saccharine tablets, vegetables and apples, eggs, even a pair of tame rabbits. We spent our days selling or raffling these things among the army chaps and buying more goods with the profits.

◀ A German guard watches Polish PoWs through the barbed wire of their prison camp.

STAN

The Germans? We got along alright. They respected you for what you were and you respected them for what they were: the governor. At work a New Zealander who spoke German was in charge of us. Over him was an old German sergeant. He was OK but his understudies could be a nuisance.

▼ A German sentry chats to PoWs during a more relaxed moment of camp life.

A few guards despised their prisoners and mistreated them by beating them or depriving them of food. The PoWs sometimes brought trouble on themselves by disrupting the camp with rowdy or uncooperative behaviour. Nevertheless, in time many PoWs developed quite amicable relationships with their captors.

LEN

In time we gradually began to see each other more and more as we really were. It seems to me that all people have the same amount of good and bad, often lurking just under the skin. In my experience there were good men among our enemy.

Keeping Busy

Locked up for years, PoWs could easily become depressed. They lost all hope of ever seeing their home, families and friends again.

To keep up spirits all kinds of entertainment were organized. These ranged from simple card games and home-made board games to sports and full-scale concerts.

BOB

The standard of entertainment was very high as many of the performers were ex-professionals. After the war some of them became famous.

▲ Bob's painting of PoWs building a theatre for camp entertainment. Entertainment was very important for keeping PoW morale high.

▲ A British PoW football team, complete with trophy and the name of their favourite team back home. Playing in army boots took some skill.

LEN

A football appeared in the camp and due to shortage of fit men I was roped in to play in a British versus Dutch match. To my surprise, we won, two goals to nil. The Japs watched the game with considerable interest, and afterwards gave each member of the winning team a packet of cigarettes and a bar of soap as prizes.

JEAN

We started a football team that played against the forced labour contingent. These were people from countries that the Nazis had conquered who had been taken to Germany and forced to work. In the summer we swam in the River Netz near the camp. Of course, the guards kept an eye on us all the time. A friend and I taught a prisoner from northern France to read since he was illiterate.

There was plenty of opportunity to study, too, although books, paper and writing materials were scarce. Learning a foreign language (especially that of the captors) was popular.

So Far from Home

The Geneva Convention said that PoWs were entitled to send and receive letters and small gifts from home. Until the last year of the war, when communications were difficult, the system worked quite well in Germany and Italy. PoWs in Japanese camps, however, received far less contact with the outside world.

JEAN

We always really looked forward to the mail, which was rationed. We were given cards to send to our families: one letter and one card per month.

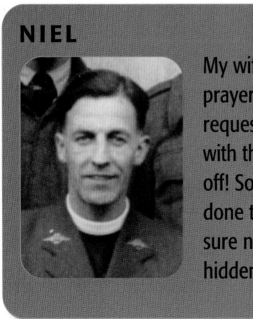

NIEL

My wife sent me a prayer book at my request. It arrived with the back torn off! Someone had done that to make sure nothing was hidden inside.

"WHAT IS IT?- OH, A PHOTO OF MY GIRL - I THINK!"

▶ A painting by Bob Coles shows PoWs enjoying their post.

STAN

We really looked forward to Red Cross parcels, especially when they had cigarettes in. Gradually they got fewer and fewer, though. Nothing was getting through.

The Red Cross also sent parcels of food, clothing and cigarettes from neutral countries like Switzerland and Sweden. As these things were often in short supply, they were sometimes stolen before they reached the PoWs.

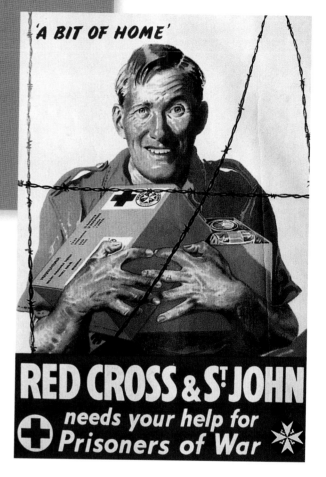

'A BIT OF HOME'

RED CROSS & St JOHN
✚ needs your help for
Prisoners of War ✠

LEN

One day I received six letters from home. The letters were all over a year old. Difficult to understand now perhaps, but that first evening all my friends, and even a dozen strangers, came to me with a whispered request to read my precious letters. Many of our men, some with a wife and children, received no mail during the whole of their captivity.

▲ A poster encourages people back home to give what they can to organizations that send parcels to PoWs. Despite the difficulties, many parcels got through.

Escape!

Until 1944, when it was clear the Axis powers were going to be defeated, many PoWs felt it was their duty to try to escape. This was especially true of airmen whose skills were badly needed in the war effort.

BOB

We had been in the hospital just two weeks when we decided to try to get away. We padded my bed with a bolster and spare pillows, so that the night nurse on her rounds might not notice our absence. I even left a note to the hospital staff who had been decent to us, saying that it was our duty to attempt an escape. I was particularly sorry for the guard...

▶ Bob's painting of how he and a colleague escaped from a Dutch hospital. They were recaptured shortly afterwards.

Those attempting escape faced two problems: getting out of the camp, and then reaching a friendly or neutral country. The first step was usually easier than the second, especially for those held by the Japanese who had to travel hundreds of kilometres through tropical rainforest. Moreover, all PoWs trying to escape risked being shot.

NIEL

We decided to make the men organize themselves into groups of ten with an NCO [lower rank officer] in charge of each group. We agreed that three long blasts on a whistle would be the sign for everyone to attack and scale the ten-foot walls round the camp simultaneously.

All hell seemed to be let loose, the men cheering and as they all stormed the walls, using bed-boards as ladders, the guards firing their machine guns. [The mass break-out was wholly successful and later it was discovered that the Italian guards had fired into the air.]

◄ Cheerful French soldiers arrive in Britain after escaping from Germany via Russia, 1941.

Freedom at Last

Liberation was usually a chaotic business. Some PoWs literally burst out of their camp. Others were set free when Allied soldiers – British, American, French or Russian – arrived. Still others were at liberty when the guards simply opened the gates and waved them out.

STAN

A German sergeant, who had been told to move us, lined us up and asked, 'Where do you want to go: to the Russians or Americans?' Most of us opted for the Americans. 'It's over there,' he said, and walked away. We went off in the direction he had been pointing.

When we reached them the Yanks were really friendly and gave us all sorts of things like chocolate – I'd forgotten what it tasted like! – and cigarettes. I was happy but sort of numb.

◀ Recently liberated British PoWs, extremely thin after living on minimal rations, tuck into their first slices of bread and butter for years.

For many, leaving the camp was not the end of their troubles. They had somehow to find their way home and come to terms with liberty after a long and difficult period of imprisonment.

JEAN

At long last – liberation! Such joy after waiting for so long. But, to our horror, we were led by our Russian liberators to Poland and then to Russia itself! We stayed there for four months, fed on bird seed, before being repatriated to France by train.

◀ US and British airmen in a PoW camp near Wetzlar, Germany, shortly after their liberation.

LEN

That evening [after being liberated] we were each given a pencil and paper and told we could write a message of not more than 20 words. It would be cabled home, we were told. I spent the whole evening trying to write a story in so few words that would be reassuring. I later found out that my parents never received it.

Coming to Terms...

Men reacted very differently to their PoW experience. Some spoke of it rarely, if at all. It was a time of horror they wished to forget. Others tried to come to terms with what they had been through by speaking about it.

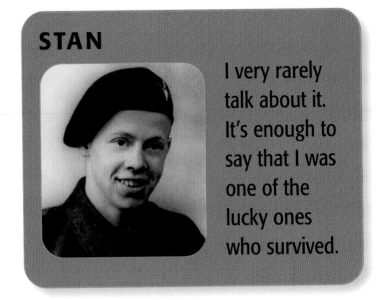

STAN

I very rarely talk about it. It's enough to say that I was one of the lucky ones who survived.

Kept – The Other Side of Tenko

L L Baynes

With a Foreword by **Ronald Searle**

Second World War PoWs wrote many books and articles about their time in captivity. These are often bitter-sweet to read. They show human beings at their most vicious but also at their most dignified and self-sacrificing.

◀ Partly to help him understand what he had been through, and partly to leave a record for others to read, Len Baynes wrote a book about his harrowing PoW experiences.

JEAN

Several years ago we had the pleasure of meeting up with former PoWs for a meal organized in several French towns. We chatted about the good and bad times we went through together. Sadly, many of them are dead now.

NIEL

There was immense relief and gratitude to have come safely through the ordeal – nothing like as bad as many, many others faced, but nevertheless, for me, quite exciting enough.

▶ In 1991, fifty years after he had crashed into the sea and been taken prisoner, Bob Coles was shown pieces of his Blenheim bomber, uncovered at the crash site.

BOB

Back home I married my fiancée who had waited for me – I still have her! I sometimes suffer sleeplessness and nightmares associated with my PoW experiences.

Glossary

Alliance agreement to fight together.

Allies alliance of Britain, France, USA, Russia and others in the Second World War.

Axis alliance of Germany, Italy and Japan in the Second World War.

Barracks housing for military personnel.

Censor cut out unwanted words or pictures.

Compound open space between buildings surrounded by a wall or fence.

Conscript compulsory calling into the armed forces.

Convent dwelling for nuns.

Dysentery serious infection of the gut.

Home Guard force set up to defend Britain against invasion during the Second World War.

Infantry foot soldiers.

Liberty freedom.

National Service compulsory period in the armed services.

Nazis the political party that was in control of Germany during the Second World War.

Neutral not belonging to either side.

PoW prisoner of War.

Raffle selling by ticket, a game of chance.

Rations basic food.

Recruit collect people to join an organization such as the army.

Red Cross an international charity.

Repatriate send home from abroad.

Saccharine artificial sweetener.

Subsistence enough to live on but no more.

Terms agreements made between the winner and the loser during the war.

Territorial Army British peace-time army of part-time volunteers.

Tommy-gun hand-held machine gun, from the name 'Thompson Machine-Gun'.

Further Reading

Non-fiction

Lancaster, Steve and Lancaster, Tony, *The Era of the Second World War (Discovering History)*, Causeway Press, 1993.

Robson, Pam and York, John, *All About the Second World War 1939-1945*, Hodder Wayland, 2002.

Ross, Stewart, *Questioning History: The Causes of World War II*, Hodder Wayland, 2003.

Resources

Books

Baynes, Len, *Kept – The Other Side of Tenko*, available from the author at 31 Mingle Lane, Stapleford, Cambridge CB2 5SY.

Reid, P.R., *The Colditz Story*, Greenwood, 1953.

Williams, Eric, *The Wooden Horse*, BBC (reprint), 1992.

Places to Visit

Imperial War Museums in Lambeth, London and Manchester are the best places to find out what life was like during the Second World War.

Index

Numbers in *italics* indicate photographs.